D1064775

LEGENDS

THE BMW BATTLE OF THE LEGENDS
1992 - 1996

DON EMDE

PRODUCTIONS

LEGENDS

THE BMW BATTLE OF THE LEGENDS
1992 - 1996

DON EMDE

DE

PRODUCTIONS

Credits

Preceding page: Mark Mitchell photo

LEGENDS. The BMW Battle of The Legends 1992 - 1996
© Don Emde 1997

All rights reserved. No part of this book may be reproduced or transmitted in any form or by any means, electronic or mechanical, including photocopying, recording, or by any information storage or retrieval system without permission from the author, except for the inclusion of brief quotations in a review.

First Printed February 1997

Manufactured in the United States of America

ISBN 0-9627434-2-9

Don Emde Productions / Infosport
30011 Ivy Glenn Drive, Suite #122
Laguna Niguel, Calif. USA 92677
Phone: 714-249-2270
Fax: 714-249-2332
E-Mail: PWRSPORT@aol.com

Layout and Design: Nancy Wegrowski.
Text: Renae Biale, Richard Dampf, Don Emde, Dain Gingerelli, Jeff Smith.
Editing: Tracy Emde, Julie Strauss.

Color Photography: Don Bok, Chuck Dearborn, DeWitt Studios, Don Emde, Tracy Emde, Greg Jarem, Mark Mitchell, Rebecca Mitchell.

Historic Photography: Dean Batchelor, Dave Friedman, Dan Mahony, Walt Mahony, B.R. Nicholls.

The publisher wishes to acknowledge and thank Renae Biale, Richard Dampf, Mick Duckworth, Dain Gingerelli, Kurt Liebmann, Mark and Rebecca Mitchell, Rob Mitchell, Reg Pridmore, Jeff Smith and Nancy Wegrowski. Without their assistance this publication would not have been possible.

About Dave Friedman photographs that appear in this book...

The entire library of Dave Friedman's motorcycle photography, as well as all publishing and reproduction rights, are owned by Don Emde. The photographs by Dave Friedman that appear in this book are used with permission.

Dedication

To the ladies who stand behind the Legends riders, event staff, AHRMA and BMW management. Without their unwavering support this series would not have been successful.

Table of Contents

Opposite page: Mark Mitchell photo

Foreword

Opposite page: Greg Jarem photo

Greg Jarem photo

BMW of North America and AHRMA were introduced to each other in November of 1990 by Jeff Glasserow of GMA. BMW was looking for some unique and unusual way to celebrate their 75th anniversary and felt vintage motor-cycle racing might work. From that intro-duction the BMW Classic Cup races were born.

The following March, 4,000 people spec-tated at the BMW Classic Cup vintage races at Daytona. Mark Polk of BMW was pleased, but he asked the question, "How can we fill the stadium?" I had always believed that great racing men would bring in crowds, because, while fans have some nostalgia for machines, the real memories center around names, char-acters, real people. Just to see those gods from the past, to hear their names over the loud speaker and finally get to meet them. This would work.

It was during a lunch meeting that I had with Jeff and Mark in October of 1991 that Glasserow threw the "IROC" auto racing concept into the conversation we were having about putting former champions into action at our events. I asked, "Would they race vintage BMW's?" "No," said Mark, "Modern ones." He went on to say, "I like it," then asked again, "but will it fill the Speedway?" First time out of the box it didn't fill the Speedway, but attendance leaped up to 16,000; the next year 20,000 and it has continued to grow. Now

instead of one cramped day, we have two cramped days and a total of 40-50,000 spec-tators. The early part of Bike Week has become as crowded as the Daytona 200 weekend.

It is a real pleasure and privilege to work with the Legends. They are, without exception, first class people. However, none of them would have achieved what they have if they were not individuals. Motorcycling is not, in the final analysis, a team game. So there are egos to contend with even in the twilight of their greatness. Old rivalries rise to the surface, hard words are exchanged from time to time, adrenalin still leaps in great gobs through their arteries as of old.

People ask, "Is it just a show?" Well, I have always asked that since they are professional that they give us a contradictory gift... excitement in a safe package. Close racing and a free-for-all at the end. These are our cham-pions from days gone by. Remember, we want to keep them, especially now, in one piece. No, it has never been a show, these guys do it for real. If the show's good, it's because they are the best.

Jeff Smith

Executive Director
American Historic Racing
Motorcycle Association

Preface

Opposite page: Greg Jarem photo

(Left to right): Tom deMange, Richard Dampf, Bud Gerber and Chuck Dearborn.

What a thrill and a privilege it has been to work so closely with some of the greatest names in motorcycling history who have participated in the BMW Battle of The Legends. And what an honor to have men like John Surtees and Geoff Duke serve as our venerable Grand Marshals. My memories of the last six years would fill pages, but here are a few that stand out in my mind:

At the 1993 Daytona event, I had the opportunity to meet Walter Zeller for the first time. The presence, smile and grace of this late-great racer is something I will always remember fondly.

An amusing memory from the same event involved our British racer Phil Read. In an attempt to get a leg up on his fellow competitors, he tried to disconnect the rev limiter on his motorcycle. Instead, he pulled off all of the coil wires, and his motorcycle would not even start just minutes before the race.

That same year, the entire fleet of motorcycles were nearly sent out of the pits for the second race with only a half-gallon of gas in the tanks. Fortunately, we caught our oversight just in time and saved ourselves from what would have been a very embarrassing situation had all 15 motorcycles run out of gas on the track!

At Mid-Ohio in 1995 we sat on the edge of our seats between racing action as we watched representatives from Forbes inflate one of their famous hot air balloons. Despite their valiant attempts and cheers of encouragement from the crowd, high winds kept their ascension plans to a minimum. In 1996, they returned to the infield for a second time, and made a picture perfect liftoff and flight out of the track.

At Daytona in 1996, PaceRider Jack Wells and his sidecar passenger Jim Lidgey were an inspirational pair. Jim had been seriously injured in a motorcycle accident while riding to Daytona the previous year and they could not participate in the PaceRide as planned. The wide smiles on their faces after they successfully completed their PaceRide laps around Daytona Speedway in 1996 made my day.

A funny moment occurred at Mid-Ohio in 1996 when some young children from a local church group lined up at the Legends autograph signing table. I recall one youngster (obviously unfamiliar with the concept of autographs) looked completely shocked when Don Emde signed her poster and demanded to know why he "wrote on it."

Of course, no program of this magnitude could be successful without the help of some very special people. This group includes my wonderful wife Pat, who has put up with my total envelopment in these events for the past six years. Other behind-the-scenes heroes include dedicated technicians Chuck Dearborn, Tom deMange, Bud Gerber and David Dampf.

I want to say thanks to our public relations representative Renae Biale of Mountain Avenue Associates and to Rob Mitchell of BMW's Corporate Communications Department for giving the series the professional look that it deserved.

I would also like to extend my heartfelt gratitude to Jeff Smith, Executive Director of the American Historic Racing Motorcycle Association (AHRMA), and his lovely wife Irene for their tireless enthusiasm and their attention to the myriad details these events have required. In fact, I am indebted to the entire AHRMA organization for their tremendous interest and encouragement.

Finally, I would like to thank Phil Capossela, Vice President of the Motorcycle Group of BMW of North America, and Scott Arigot, National Marketing Manager of the Motorcycle Group, for their confidence and support in allowing me to manage the BMW Battle of the Legends. This event has been, without a doubt, the highlight of my career with BMW.

Richard Dampf

National Event Manager
BMW of North America

DeWitt Studio photo.

Introduction

THE BEST SEAT IN THE HOUSE

For me, the BMW Battle of The Legends began in the Fall of 1991. It had been over 15 fairly tranquil years since I had hung up my racing leathers when I got a call one day from Jeff Smith, the Executive Director of the American Historic Racing Motorcycle Association. His first words were, "Don, I've got an offer that you can't refuse." He then went on tell me how he had arranged an event for the upcoming Daytona Bike Week. There, hopefully, I along with nine other riders of days-gone-by would race identical factory-prepared BMW's in a kind of match race to be held during AHRMA's vintage day at the Daytona International Speedway. Jeff explained that the concept of the event was to showcase racers of the past who had all accomplished big things during their racing days. In a matter of days, Jeff had me and nine others signed up for his new program and the BMW Battle of The Legends was born.

Now, just over five years later, my publishing company was asked by BMW of North America to produce this book on the series that has taken us to both coasts and put us in front of crowds totalling some 200,000-plus racing fans.

Where normally the journalist is on the outside of the track watching the events unfold, in this case I have been right there side by side with the likes of Yvon Duhamel, Gary Nixon and the rest of the Legends every mile of the way. I'd have to say I've had the best seat in the house. Hopefully, this rather unorthodox link of publisher to subject matter

Few journalists ever get the view of the action that I did in the BMW Battle of The Legends series.

will add to the perspective that you'll gain from the book.

But first let's go back to the beginning. How did the BMW Battle of The Legends series come to be? To begin with, there has been quite an increase in interest in vintage motorcycles in the last decade. Like all other forms of motorcycling, it did not take long before someone came up with the idea of

racing them. AHRMA, which stands for the American Historic Racing Motorcycle Association, is an organization created to establish a organized structure for vintage motorcycle racing. The association has written a rule book covering classes for just about any old motorcycle, established representatives around the country and set up an event calendar and national point system.

While there had previously been a couple of people talking about "Legend-type" competitions, the ones that actually made one happen are Jeff Glasserow, Jeff Smith and Mark Polk. Glasserow's company, GMA, does marketing consulting and has BMW of North America as a client. As it turns out, he is also an AHRMA member and sponsors a rider named Rusty Lowry in vintage racing.

In the Summer of 1990, Jeff Smith was hired by AHRMA as its Executive Director. Jeff is himself a two-time World Motocross champion, so he knows a thing or two about big time racing and legendary achievements. About the same time, Jeff Glasserow had gotten the attention of BMW's Mark Polk about the growth of vintage racing and was recommending that BMW get involved in some way.

Not long after taking the reins at AHRMA, Smith, with the assistance of Glasserow, got BMW of North America to expand its involvement to become a sponsor of the 1991 Daytona vintage races and annual AHRMA awards banquet. That year's attendance of roughly 4,000 fans was proof to BMW that there was great potential in vintage events. But Polk felt the event could be significantly bigger, a point that both Smith and Glasserow agreed with. He expressed BMW's interest to Glasserow in getting even more involved, but said he wasn't sure how to do it.

Glasserow told Jeff Smith about BMW's interest in getting more involved with AHRMA. Glasserow asked Smith to come to New Jersey and meet with him and Mark Polk. Jeff Smith soon was on a plane to New Jersey and the three had a lengthy lunch meeting to go over a plan for 1992 and beyond.

Jeff Smith's philosophy is that AHRMA is a members-driven organization and needs to focus on events for its members to use their vintage motorcycles. He felt that there was the potential to draw large crowds of spectators to AHRMA events, but that personalities would

Mark Mitchell photo

be the draw needed, not the machines themselves.

In the lunch meeting the idea of the International Race Of Champions (IROC) race car series came up and the seed of the idea of the Battle of The Legends was planted. When it was suggested that motorcycle racing legends take part in an "IROC" style event, Smith remembers saying, "You mean all on vintage BMW's?" The answer from Polk and Glasserow was, "No, on modern ones."

The three proceeded to hammer out a rough plan and Glasserow and Polk got BMW management very excited and ultimately committed to such an event.

The next step was to figure out who could (or would) participate in such an event? Jeff Smith called Dick Mann and myself, both former BSA team riders (as was Smith on the motocross side) to start creating a list. The key was to pick riders that people would want to come see race, and who were either interested and/or in a position to ride well enough to put on a good show.

While there were a few on the initial list that didn't want to get back on the race track, Dick, myself and the eight others that ultimately came to Daytona in 1992 thought it would be great fun. And we were right.

Being somewhat goal oriented, I set three goals that have guided me through all nine of the events that have been held through 1996...be safe, have fun and beat more guys than beat me. I figured if I could stay in the saddle and end up in the middle of the pack somewhere I could have a great time. Except for one spin out on a warm up lap at Daytona back in 1995, my plan has worked pretty well.

The Battle of The Legends format is pretty simple. Since most AHRMA races are at least two day events, the Legends races are divided so that we have a race on each day and then Olympic-type scoring is used to award an overall winner for that event.

Along the way, there have been some changes in machinery and race tracks. There have been a few new riders invited to join the series at certain races, and a few sat out for a race or two. In all, twenty-three legends of the past took part in at least one race.

BMW and AHRMA never wanted things to get too serious, but I can tell you that every one of the Legends riders has too much of a winning spirit in them still to just sit back and

let everyone blow by. It has been a lot of fun to go at it just like we did years ago.

Often, I would get distracted watching someone like Gary Nixon get really deep into a turn and dive under Duhamel or Aldana and I would find myself watching when I should have been racing. A few times I found myself having such a great time observing the action that I didn't get on the gas fast enough and lost a few bike lengths.

Along the way, I have had some moments on the track that I feel pretty good about. I was able to pull off a win at one of the two Mid-Ohio races both in 1995 and 1996. It sure felt great to come across the line and get that checkered flag first after all these years!

Off the track, we have all had a good time too. It was pretty neat to have guys like John Surtees, Geoff Duke, Phil Read, Walter Villa, Walter Zeller and Hugh Anderson come to Daytona. These were names that I had read about as I was growing up and, with the exception of Read, had never met.

Probably the most unexpected result that I think all of the riders experienced was the "royal treatment" that we received at every event. At Daytona in 1992 George Roeder made the comment that he "never got treated so good back when he was racing for a living!" That pretty much summed up the reaction that we all had.

I know that I speak for all the riders who rode in the series when I say thanks to everyone at BMW of North America for giving us the chance to come back to the sport and have a little time in the spotlight. We are especially grateful to Richard Dampf and all his assistants who worked so hard behind the scenes to prepare our bikes. Thanks to the people at Metzeler Tires for giving us some great tires to ride on. Thanks to Jeff Smith and everyone at AHRMA for organizing the events. Thanks to the people at the Daytona International Speedway and also at Loudon, Sears Point and Mid-Ohio for having us. Lastly, thanks to all the fans who have come out to our events and made us feel special again. We hope you enjoyed watching the show as much as we did putting it on. Ride safe.

Don Emde

Mark Mitchell photo

LEGENDS

JOHN SURTEES

GEOFF DUKE

DAVID ALDANA

HUGH ANDERSON

MARK BRELSFORD

DON CASTRO

CHRIS DRAAYER

YVON DUHAMEL

DON EMDE

WALT FULTON

DICK KLAMFOTH

KURT LIEBMANN

DICK MANN

BART MARKEL

EDDIE MULDER

JODY NICHOLAS

GARY NIXON

REG PRIDMORE

PHIL READ

ROGER REIMAN

GEORGE ROEDER

JAY SPRINGSTEEN

DON VESCO

WALTER VILLA

WALTER ZELLER

Battle of the Legends

Racing

PROFILES

JOHN SURTEES

Following fellow Englishman Geoff Duke's lead, John Surtees signed with an Italian manufacturer to contest the Grand Prix series in Europe in 1956. Surtees didn't let the MV Augusta team down, either, winning the 500cc world championship that season. Surtees eventually won six more world titles for MV before another Italian manufacturer signed him. This time it was Ferrari, who hired Surtees to drive in the prestigious Formula One auto racing championship. By 1964, Surtees and Ferrari had a world title to share with Surtees becoming the first - and still only - person to win both the motorcycle and automobile world titles. A few years later Surtees formed his own automobile race team, and hired yet another former motorcycle GP legend— Mike Hailwood— to drive for him. During the past 10 years Surtees has maintained a high profile throughout motorcycle racing, including Emeritus standing with the BMW Battle of the Legends. He was the official Grand Marshal at Daytona in 1994 and 1995.

Surtees at speed on his 350cc MV Agusta at the Ulster Grand Prix in 1959.

B. R. Nicholls

Winner of 3 350cc Grand Prix World Championships (1958, 1959, 1960)
Winner of 4 500cc Grand Prix World Championships (1956, 1958,1959, 1960)
1964 Formula One Grand Prix World Champion (automobiles)

Mark Mitchell

1996

Grand Marshal

PROFILES

GEOFF DUKE

When students of Grand Prix road racing speak of Geoff Duke, they do so in reverence. For the Englishman is considered one of the true masters of the sport. Having won three world titles for the Norton factory team during the early years of Grand Prix world championship racing, Duke did the unthinkable for an Englishman at the time— he agreed to ride for a foreign marque, in this case the Italian Gilera factory team. Duke's reasoning was that if you couldn't beat them, then join them. He had relinquished his 500cc world crown to Gilera's Umberto Masetti in 1952, but regained the title for 1953 and 1954 as a Gilera rider. In his career, he won 87 Grand Prix races, including 6 Isle of Man TT events. The BMW Battle of the Legends wouldn't be complete without a legend such as Geoff Duke, and so he was awarded the honor of Grand Marshal for the BMW Battle of the Legends at Daytona in 1996.

Geoff flies over Ballaugh Bridge on his BMW at the 1958 Isle of Man Senior TT.

B. R. Nicholls

Winner of 2 350cc Grand Prix World Championships (1951, 1952)

Winner of 4 500cc Grand Prix World Championships (1951, 1953, 1954, 1955)

Mark Mitchell

PROFILES

DAVID ALDANA

David Aldana is perhaps one of the most versatile racers of all time. He won three AMA Grand National races for the BSA factory team in 1970, and he also was a member of that manufacturer's U.S. motocross team in 1971. Following the demise of the BSA marque, Aldana rode for Norton during the early '70s, becoming a dominant rider at Ascot Park with the agile British twin-cylinder bike. He was one of the original U.S.A. team members in the Anglo-American Match Series of 1971, and later joined the U.S. Suzuki road race team. Aldana competed as a privateer on a Yamaha TZ750 for a number of years before specializing in endurance road racing for Team Suzuki in the early '80s. And, finally, as a member of the Legends team, Aldana won more races— four— than any other rider in the BMW-backed series. Aldana's race track legacy certainly will be his longevity, coupled with an uncanny ability to win at all forms of motorcycle racing.

Aldana won the 1970 Talladega 200-mile road race riding a BSA three-cylinder 750.

Dave Friedman

Here he shows the aggressive style that won him three AMA Nationals in 1970.

Dave Friedman

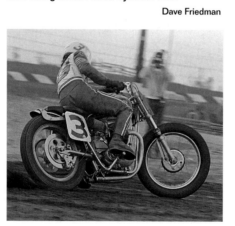

David was a threat at any race, including this TT event at Ascot Park in 1971.

Dave Friedman

In his career David raced for the BSA, Suzuki and Norton factories.

Dave Friedman

Winner of 4 AMA Grand National races

Winner of Suzuka Eight Hour

Opposite page: Mark Mitchell photo

Greg Jarem

PROFILES

HUGH ANDERSON

Although he raced virtually every size and type of roadrace motorcycle in his career, Hugh Anderson made a name for himself racing small-bore two-strokes for the Suzuki factory team in Europe more than 30 years ago. In addition to winning 27 National Championships in his native country, he highlighted his career in 1963, scoring a double-world championship, winning the 50cc and 125cc classes that year. He finished atop the world standings again in 1964 (50cc) and 1965 (125cc). After retiring from active racing, the friendly New Zealander took up vintage road racing, scoring several classic-bike championships in Europe. Hugh Anderson was a class act in the 1960s, as well as in his solo performance in 1993 as a member of the Legends race team at Daytona. Today Hugh is an active collector of vintage and classic motorcycles.

A youthful Hugh Anderson at Brands Hatch in England in 1962.

B. R. Nicholls

Suzuki-mounted Anderson en route to a third place finish in the 125cc class at the Isle of Man in 1966.

B. R. Nicholls

Best known for his rides on 50cc and 125cc machines, Hugh also rode big bikes, as seen here on a 350cc AJS.

B. R. Nicholls

Hugh at speed on his exotic "works" Suzuki at the 1964 Isle of Man TT.

Dean Batchelor

Winner of 2 125cc Grand Prix World Championships (1963, 1965)

Winner of 2 50cc Grand Prix World Championships (1963, 1964)

4 British Championships   27 New Zealand National Championships

Opposite page: Mark Mitchell photo

Mark Mitchell

PROFILES

MARK BRELSFORD

Mark Brelsford joined the AMA Expert ranks in 1969, and during his first four seasons, won at least one Grand National race every year. On the way to his AMA Grand National championship in 1972 Brelsford won three races, the most ever for him in a single season. The California-native was clearly a young man with a promising future in motorcycle racing. Then, tragically, the following year his racing career was put in jeopardy, first by a fiery crash at Daytona which severely damaged his hand, followed by a life-threatening crash on the half-mile dirt track at Columbus, Ohio in 1974. Although he was not able to return to active racing following the Columbus crash, the former Harley-Davidson factory team rider clearly left his mark on the racing world. Brelsford's first return to the race track since 1974 came at the Mid-Ohio round of the BMW Battle of The Legends race in 1995.

Mark muscles his Harley-Davidson "iron barrel" XR750 around the Ascot Park TT track in 1971.
Dave Friedman

Unleashing the full power of his factory-Harley-Davidson XR750 at Louisville, Ky.
Dave Friedman

Mark won the Ascot TT National three times in his career.
Dave Friedman

A versatile racer, Mark won the Loudon, NH 100-mile National road race in 1971.
Dave Friedman

1972 AMA Grand National Champion

Winner of 7 AMA Grand National races

Opposite page: Mark Mitchell photo

Mark Mitchell

DON CASTRO

Don Castro made headlines in 1969 when he and his arch rival David Aldana battled all year long for supremacy of the AMA Amateur division on the national circuit. He was considered a versatile racer when he rode for the Triumph and Yamaha factory teams during the early 1970s, competitive on both dirt track and road race bikes. He placed fifth in the 1970 AMA Grand National Championship riding for Triumph, his rookie year on the circuit. In 1974 he won an AMA dirt track national for Yamaha, in the process helping that factory win its second of four AMA Manufacturer's Championships. That same season Castro also won a dazzling duel with his Yamaha teammate, Kenny Roberts, during the Daytona 250cc race. The win aboard the lightweight two-stroke proved once again that Castro was a racer who could win on asphalt as well as dirt. And now, as a member of the Legends team, Castro's versatility has spread to production-based race bikes.

Don finished 2nd in the 1970 Daytona 200 on a factory-prepared Triumph 750.

Dave Friedman

He was a factor at all AMA Nationals his rookie year, finishing 5th in the national points.

Dave Friedman

In 1974 he upset Kenny Roberts to win the 100-mile lightweight race at Daytona.

Dave Friedman

After racing for the Triumph factory through 1971, he joined the factory Yamaha team.

Dave Friedman

Winner of 1973 AMA San Jose Half-Mile

Winner of the 1974 AMA Daytona 250cc Lightweight road race

Opposite page: Greg Jarem photo

24

Chuck Dearborn

PROFILES

CHRIS DRAAYER

In 1966 Chris Draayer finished fifth in the AMA Grand National standings, and was voted AMA Rookie of the Year. Almost overnight he had established himself as one of racing's future stars. Then, the following season while in contention for the coveted No. 1 Plate he crashed badly, sustaining a broken neck and legs, massive internal injuries, and the loss of his left arm. It forced Draayer into retirement from professional racing. A man who many race enthusiasts at the time had pegged as a future AMA Grand National champion returned to his home in Utah, where he settled into a career in real estate. The injuries didn't end Draayer's desire to race, however, and he eventually returned to competition in sportsman off-road events. He joined the Legends team for the 1995 Mid-Ohio and 1996 Daytona races. Once again Chris Draayer was racing among champions.

Chris hugs the fence at the old Sacramento Fairgrounds Mile track in 1966.

Dan Mahony

In his Amateur year, Harley-mounted Draayer was successful at California's Ascot Park.

Dan Mahony

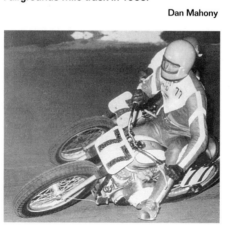

In 1966 he nearly won an Expert main at Ascot, a rare feat for a non-California rider.

Dan Mahony

Draayer shows the style that took him to 5th in the National points in 1966.

Dan Mahony

1966 AMA Rookie of the Year

Opposite page: Mark Mitchell photo

Greg Jarem

P R O F I L E S

YVON DUHAMEL

Canada's Yvon Duhamel made history in 1968 on a 350cc Yamaha when he became the first man to qualify for the Daytona 200 at over 150 mph. Although he never won the Daytona 200, he scored wins in the 250cc Lightweight race at the famous superspeedway in 1968 and 1969 riding Yamaha 250s. In all, Duhamel started the Daytona 200 14 times, riding Yamahas and later factory-built Kawasaki 500 and 750 triples. He was especially dominant in AMA road racing during the 1973 season, having been the lap-leader at every race, winning two (Charlotte and Ontario) in the process. And while this famous legend never won the prestigious Daytona 200, his son Miguel has finished first there twice— 1991 and 1996. As a member of the Legends team, the senior Duhamel made history one more time at Daytona International Speedway— he won the first BMW Battle of the Legends race in 1992.

Yvon was 2nd in the 1968 Daytona 200 riding for Canada's Yamaha distributor Trev Deeley.

Dave Friedman

Known primarily as a road racer, he competed in many dirt track races in the 1960's.

Dave Friedman

In 1971 he gave Kawasaki its first-ever national victory when he won Talladega.

Dave Friedman

The hard charging Canadian won the last two road races of 1973 on a Kawasaki.

Dave Friedman

**Winner of 5 AMA Grand National road races
Winner of first BMW Battle of the Legends race in 1992**

Opposite page: Mark Mitchell photo

Mark Mitchell

P R O F I L E S

DON EMDE

If you're going to win a race, you might as well make it the biggest, most important event on the calendar. That's exactly what San Diego-native Don Emde did in 1972, becoming the first man to win the Daytona 200 with a two-stroke-powered motorcycle. In fact, his ride aboard Mel Dinesen's privateer Yamaha 350 started a string of 13 successive Daytona 200 wins for Yamaha that lasted until 1985 when Freddie Spencer put his Honda NSR500 in Victory Circle. Emde's Daytona win also marked the first— and so far only— time that the prestigious 200-mile road race has been won by two members of the same family; his father, the late Floyd Emde, rode an Indian to victory at the original "beach course" in 1948. Don, one of the original BMW Battle of The Legends team members, won one of the two races at the 1996 Mid-Ohio Legends event and finished second overall. Today he manages his own publishing company.

Don won the 1970 100-mile 250cc race at Talladega over Gary Nixon and Cal Rayborn.
Dave Friedman

He raced dirt track events on BSA and later, Harley-Davidson, as seen at Louisville in 1972.
Dave Friedman

Riding for the BSA factory team in 1971, he was ranked third that year in AMA road racing.
Dave Friedman

Emde won the 1972 Daytona 200 on a privately-entered 350cc Yamaha TR-3.
Dave Friedman

Winner of the 1972 Daytona 200 road race

Member of U.S. Team at 1971 & 1972 Transatlantic Match Races

Opposite page: Mark Mitchell photo

Mark Mitchell

WALT FULTON

Like many racers, Walt Fulton started competing at an early age. He was 15 years old when he entered his first race and within a few years he was competing on the national level. He won the novice race at Daytona in 1967 after passing the entire field to win from the back of the pack. The following year, as an AMA Expert, the young rider from California won the Heidelberg National road race. Indeed, Fulton's consistency on asphalt tracks helped label him as a road race specialist. His reputation was well-founded when, in 1970, he was the only Harley-Davidson rider to finish that year's grueling Daytona 200. His racing career complete, Fulton joined the staff as technical editor for *Cycle Guide*, and later *Cycle World* magazine. His engineering background ultimately led to his most recent profession as an expert witness for an engineering firm.

Riding for the Harley-Davidson factory, Fulton won the 1968 Heidelberg, PA National.

Dave Friedman

He also rode prepared Kawasaki in the 250 class at Daytona in 1968.

Dave Friedman

1970 was a tough year at Daytona for Harley-Davidsons. Only Fulton's was around at the finish.

Dave Friedman

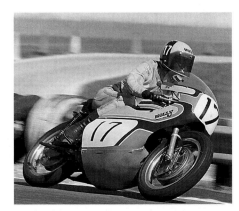

In 1971 Walt rode on a 500cc Kawasaki.

Dave Friedman

Winner of the 1967 AMA Daytona 250cc Novice road race

Winner of the 1968 AMA Heidelberg National road race

Opposite page: Mark Mitchell photo

Greg Jarem

DICK KLAMFOTH

You might say that Ohio's Dick Klamfoth was a pioneer of modern-day American racing, because when racing resumed after World War II he was one of the first to recognize the potential of the lightweight English-made bikes such as Norton and BSA. In fact, Klamfoth was the first rider to win the Daytona 200 three times. His wins were accomplished aboard a Norton Manx prepared by the legendary tuner Francis Beart of Isle of Man fame. He also finished second once riding a factory-prepared twin-cylinder BSA. Klamfoth's decision to ride something other than Harley-Davidson or Indian bikes— the brand of choice for most riders back then— resulted in 12 AMA Grand National race wins, including five road races and seven half-mile dirt track events. Even though Klamfoth was awarded Legends Emeritus status, he competed in the third event— the 1993 Loudon, New Hampshire BMW Battle of The Legends race— where he placed seventh overall.

A great dirt-tracker, Dick won seven AMA half-mile Nationals riding a BSA Gold Star.

Don Emde Collection

Dick zooms down the beach on a factory BSA in 1954. He finished 2nd to Bobby Hill.

Don Emde Collection

In addition to his success at Daytona, Klamfoth won the 100-mile Laconia Road Race twice.

Don Emde Collection

Fresh off the bike after winning the 1949 Daytona 200, the first of his three wins.

Don Emde Collection

Winner of 12 AMA Grand National races

Winner of 3 Daytona 200s (1949, 1951, 1952)

Opposite page: Mark Mitchell photo

Greg Jarem

PROFILES

KURT LIEBMANN

I t was only fitting that Kurt Liebmann would one day join the BMW Battle of The Legends team. After all, the racer from New Jersey had a long history of racing specially tuned BMWs built by his father, the late Oscar Liebmann. He competed in Canadian and American east coast sportsman road races, as well as numerous AMA National road races such as Daytona, Loudon and Road Atlanta. And, as an experienced machinist himself, Liebmann had developed a reputation for his expertise in fabricating specialty parts for the boxer-twin motors; he was even called upon by the fabled Butler & Smith organization to provide special parts for that team's juggernaut superbike effort of the mid-1970s. And through Butler & Smith's effort— and the support of people such as Kurt Liebmann— BMW scored the first-ever AMA Superbike win at Daytona in 1976. For Kurt Liebmann, racing BMWs is more than a way of life— it's a tradition.

Kurt was a pioneer in the development of the BMW twin as a competitive road racer.

Dave Friedman

Kurt won at the 1984 and 1985 Daytona vintage races on the "Oscar Liebmann Special" BMW RS-500 Rennsport.   Don Bok

He still campaigns the same Honda CR750 in vintage events that he rode back in the 1970's.

Mark Mitchell

Legend versus Legend, Ducati-mounted Liebmann leads Roger Reiman at the 1990 Daytona vintage events.   Don Bok

1961 Canadian 200cc Road Race Champion

First AMA Victory in America on a Honda - 1962

1996 AHRMA-BMW Classic Cup Champion F-750 & F-Vintage

Opposite page: Greg Jarem photo

Greg Jarem

PROFILES

DICK MANN

I f somebody were to describe the quintessential AMA Grand National Champion, the name Dick Mann would enter the picture. Beyond his two Grand National titles and two dozen race wins, Mann was a gutsy racer who generally built and tuned his own racing bikes. Often plagued by bad luck, that all changed in 1970 when he became the first rider to win the Daytona 200 aboard a Japanese-made bike. He won the "200" that year to help Honda debut its new four-cylinder CB750. The following year he won his second Daytona 200 and Grand National title riding for the BSA factory. Mann was the first rider to win in all five categories of racing— Road Racing, Mile, Half-Mile, Shorttrack and TT (Kenny Roberts is the only other rider to accomplish this feat). Following his retirement from professional racing, Mann competed in sportsman and vintage events, and was even a member of the U.S. ISDE team. He competed in the first BMW Battle of the Legends race in 1992.

One of the all-time best dirt track racers, Dick Mann slides his BSA Gold Star.

Dave Friedman

Dick made history in 1970 when he became the first to win the Daytona 200 on a Honda.

Dave Friedman

Dick won four AMA Nationals in 1971 and won the Grand National Championship.

Dave Friedman

In 1971 Dick repeated his 1970 Daytona win, taking the win this time for the BSA factory.

Dave Friedman

AMA Grand National Champion (1963, 1971)
Winner of 24 AMA Grand National races
Winner of 2 Daytona 200s (1970, 1971)

Opposite page: Greg Jarem photo

Greg Jarem

PROFILES

BART MARKEL

Racers back in the 1960s called him Bad Bart. For good reason— Bart Markel of Flint, Michigan would just as soon stuff you into a black hole in space than to let you beat him. Consequently, "Bad Bart" personified the champion's champion on his way to winning 28 AMA Grand National races (more than any other racer at the time) and three AMA Grand National titles. A worthy road racer, Markel was best known for his expertise as an aggressive dirt tracker who never gave up. He could race with the best of them in all conditions, and capped wins at Mile, Half-Mile, TT and Shorttrack events. His first National win was at the 1960 Peoria TT, an event he would win five times. He also won 18 Nationals on half-mile tracks with his final victory coming at Columbus 11 years after that first win at Peoria. Bart raced in the first three Legends races and is now a Legends Emeritus.

Primarily a dirt tracker, he leads TT ace Skip Van Leeuwen here at Loudon in 1968.

Dave Friedman

Bart enjoyed the support of the Harley-Davidson factory for many years.

Dave Friedman

Markel was one of the most aggressive motorcycle racers in American history.

Dave Friedman

He won 28 AMA Nationals, his last coming in 1971 at Columbus, Ohio.

Dave Friedman

AMA Grand National Champion (1962, 1965, 1966)

Winner of 28 AMA Grand National races

Opposite page: Greg Jarem photo

Mark Mitchell

PROFILES

EDDIE MULDER

Few racers were as colorful as Eddie Mulder. The flamboyant rider from Southern California earned a reputation for his craftiness on two-wheels, and he never backed down. Eddie first made national news when he won the prestigious 1960 Big Bear Gran Prix at age 16. In doing so he beat literally hundreds of experienced motorcycle desert racers. Mulder's specialty in pro racing was at TT events. Riding Triumphs, he was the master at the legendary Ascot Park for many years, and all five of his AMA Grand National race wins were at TT tracks. In fact, Mulder dominated all three of the TT races on the AMA Grand National schedule during the 1966 season. While best known for TT racing, Mulder was a factor at half-mile and Mile events in the late 1960's and early '70's. He also competed in road racing on an occasional basis. Mulder's racing career ended in the 1970s when he became a Hollywood stunt man. His specialty? Motorcycles, of course.

Triumph West versus Triumph East. He leads Chuck Palmgren at the Santa Rosa Mile.

Dave Friedman

Eddie won all of the major TT Nationals of his era - Peoria, Ascot, Castle Rock and Santa Fe.

Dave Friedman

Known for his success on TT tracks, Eddie also placed high at many flattrack races.

Dave Friedman

Eddie hustles his 650cc Triumph around the TT course at Ascot, his home track.

Dave Friedman

Winner of 5 AMA Grand National races

Opposite page: Mark Mitchell photo

Mark Mitchell

P R O F I L E S

JODY NICHOLAS

here were four road races on the AMA Grand National calendar in 1963 and Jody Nicholas won two of them riding a BSA Gold Star. His win at the old Laconia track was especially notable after he fell off on the final lap and had to re-pass Harley-Davidson rider George Roeder to take the win. Practically overnight the young rider from Nashville, Tennessee, had established himself as a star. Shortly after, Nicholas became a fighter pilot in the U.S. Navy. Following his military discharge, he returned to racing motorcycles on the west coast. He rode for the Suzuki factory team during the early '70s, and if that company's potent 750cc triple had proven to be as reliable as it was fast, Nicholas certainly would have added more AMA National wins to his record. Following his retirement from professional racing Nicholas joined *Cycle World* magazine as the staff's primary road test editor. Jody particiapted in the 1995 Daytona and 1996 Mid-Ohio BMW Battle of The Legends events.

Jody finished third at the 100-mile Loudon road race in 1968 on a 350cc Yamaha.

Dave Friedman

He raced for the Suzuki factory on 250cc and 500cc twins and, later, 750cc triples.

Dave Friedman

Jody won many races at the Ascot 1/2 mile on a Norton 750 in the early 1970's.

Dave Friedman

Jody's victory of the 1972 Atlanta road race was later disallowed due to a technicality.

Dave Friedman

Winner of 2 AMA Grand National road races

Member of U.S. Team at 1972 Transatlantic Match Races

Opposite page: Mark Mitchell photo

Greg Jarem

GARY NIXON

It's safe to say that there's probably not a more determined motorcycle racer in the world than Gary Nixon. He won his first AMA Grand National race (Windber road race) in 1963, and concluded his career with a win at Loudon in 1974. For years Nixon was affiliated with the Triumph factory team, but when that company withdrew from racing the Maryland-based rider was quickly snatched up by Kawasaki, and later Suzuki, to ride their potent three-cylinder 750s in AMA road races. Nixon didn't let either team down, posting three wins for Kawasaki in '73, and the Loudon victory for Suzuki the following season. Due to a controversial decision by the FIM, Nixon was declared the runner-up in the first-ever Formula 750 World Championship in 1976. Nixon suffered many serious injuries during his career as a rider, but always returned, often more competitive than ever. He added yet another victory to his record in 1995 when he took the overall honors at the Daytona Battle of the Legends.

Gary won both the 250cc lightweight race and the "200" at Daytona in 1967.

Dave Friedman

Nixon was the 1967 and 1968 AMA Grand National Champion riding for Triumph.

Dave Friedman

He led the 1970 Daytona 200 on a 3-cylinder Triumph until the motor broke.

Dave Friedman

He later won races for both Suzuki and Kawasaki. He is seen here at Ontario in 1973.

Dave Friedman

AMA Grand National Champion (1967, 1968)
Winner of 19 AMA Grand National races
Winner of 1967 Daytona 200

Opposite page: Mark Mitchell photo

Greg Jarem

REG PRIDMORE

Reg Pridmore first raced motorcycles in his home country, England, and later resumed at the club level when he moved to America. In addition to his experience on two wheels, Reg competed for many years as a "pilot" in motorcycle sidecar racing. His first effort at big time racing in the United States was at the AMA road race Nationals in the early 1970's. When AMA Superbike racing got its start a few years later, Reg was at the forefront— literally. And, riding for the Butler & Smith BMW team, Pridmore scored the first-ever AMA Superbike Championship. He won the title the following year, riding a Kawasaki KZ1000, and managed a three-peat in '78 on the same bike. Today the expatriated Englishman owns and operates CLASS, a motorcycle riding school where he teaches safety skills and riding tips at many leading racetracks around the country. His son Jason is today one of the rising stars in American motorcycle roadracing.

Reg speeds his Kawasaki around Sears Point in 1978 en route to his third AMA Superbike title.
Craig Vetter

Reg piloted a motorcycle sidecar for many years in road race competition.
Reg Pridmore Collection

Pridmore won his first of three AMA Superbike titles in 1976 riding for BMW.
Dave Friedman

Reg developed his BMWs at AMA road race Nationals in the early to mid-1970s.
Dave Friedman

AMA Superbike Champion (1976, 1977)

1978 AMA Superbike Champion

Opposite page: Mark Mitchell photo

Greg Jarem

P R O F I L E S

PHIL READ

Throughout the 1960s Phil Read was the number one rider for the Yamaha factory road race team in Europe. As a result, he gave the tuning-fork company five Grand Prix world titles before switching to the Italian-based MV Augusta factory team in 1973, where he replaced the affable legend Giacomo Agostini. Ironically, Agostini had left MV to accept a ride for Yamaha on its new 500cc vee-four. Perhaps "Ago" left too soon, because Read and MV won two 500cc world titles together while the Yamaha team struggled, finally winning the title in 1975. In between Grand Prix racing, Read competed in many other international meets as a member of the John Player-sponsored Norton factory team. In 1972 he came to Daytona and finished fourth on one of the team's fast running four stroke twins. Read's only Legends ride was at the 1993 Daytona race where he finished a respectable fifth overall.

Read won five FIM World titles racing for the Yamaha factory. He is seen here at the Isle of Man.
Dean Batchelor

He came to Daytona in 1968. Riding a 350cc Yamaha he experienced motor trouble.
Dave Friedman

Phil won the 500cc World Championships in 1973 and 1974 riding MV Agustas.
Dave Friedman

Read came back to Daytona in 1972 and finished fourth on a John Player Norton.
Dave Friedman

Winner of 2 500cc Grand Prix World Championships (1973, 1974)

Winner of 4 250cc Grand Prix World Championships (1964, 1965, 1968, 1971)

Winner of 1 125cc Grand Prix World Championship (1968)

Opposite page: Mark Mitchell photo

Mark Mitchell

PROFILES

ROGER REIMAN

Ageless might be the best word to describe 58-year-old Roger Reiman; he was fast on a bike in 1964 when he won the No. 1 Plate, and he's fast today as a vintage bike racer and Legends competitor. His best finish in a Legends race was a second at the 1995 Mid-Ohio event. Reiman should feel especially comfortable racing one of the BMW Legends bikes on Daytona Speedway's 31-degree banking, too. After all, he won the prestigious Daytona 200 three times, making him the third of only five riders ever to do so (Actually, he was the first to win three on the Superspeedway; Dick Klamfoth and Brad Andres won on the old "beach course"; Kenny Roberts and Scott Russell also have won three on the paved track.). In addition to his success in road racing, Roger won the 1964 short track National at Hinsdale, Illinois. When Reiman's not competing on the track today, he usually can be found at his Harley-Davidson dealership in Kewanee, Illinois.

Roger slides his Harley-Davidson KR around the Portland Mile just ahead of California rider Mel Lacher in 1968.   Dave Friedman

Consistent finishes in dirt track racing helped Roger win the 1964 AMA Number One Plate.   Dave Friedman

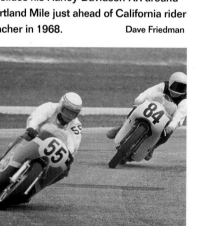

Reiman was the first rider to win three Daytona 200's at the Daytona International Speedway.   Dave Friedman

Known as a Harley-Davidson rider, Reiman did ride Hondas in roadracing in 1972 and 1973.   Dave Friedman

1964 AMA Grand National Champion

Winner of 4 AMA Grand National races

Winner of 3 Daytona 200s (1961, 1964, 1965)

Opposite page: Mark Mitchell photo

Greg Jarem

P R O F I L E S

GEORGE ROEDER

George Roeder seems to always have a smile on his face, which helps explain why, as a racer back in the '60s, he was twice voted Most Popular Rider by his peers. The Ohio rider wasn't such a nice guy to his competitors on the track, though, and he won 8 AMA Grand National dirt track races— 5 on the half-miles, 3 on the miles, including a 50-lap race at the legendary Springfield Mile. Roeder's ability to coax speed out of a bike was one of the reasons that Dick O'Brien, Harley-Davidson's race team manager at the time, selected him to pilot a specially-designed 250cc Harley-Davidson single for a Land Speed Record at Bonneville in 1965. Roeder didn't let his employer down, either, setting a 176 mph record for the streamlined class. Most recently Roeder's involvement in racing includes tuning for his two sons in the Grand National and Harley-Davidson 883 Series. He also owns and operates a Harley-Davidson dealership in Ohio.

George won three AMA nationals in 1963, but lost the title to Dick Mann by one point.

Dan Mahony

George, one of the first to race with multi-color leathers, is seen here at Ascot.

Dan Mahony

Roeder was fast on mile tracks. He won Springfield in 1963 and Sacramento in 1963 and 1967.

Dan Mahony

He retired from racing briefly in the late-sixties, then returned in 1970 for one season.

Dave Friedman

Winner of 8 AMA Grand National races

250cc Land Speed Record Holder (176 mph; 1965)

Opposite page: Greg Jarem photo

Mark Mitchell

P R O F I L E S

JAY SPRINGSTEEN

One of the most unique dirt track racers of all time is Jay Springsteen. He's won in all four types of dirt track events (Mile, Half-Mile, TT and Shorttrack), and he was the first rider to accumulate 40 wins in a career. Only a mysterious stomach ailment that he developed in 1979 prevented him from winning the No. 1 Plate a fourth time. His racing career after that was sporadic, and his 40th win occurred in 1985 at the Syracuse Mile— 10 years after his first-ever win. But Springer (as he is known by his peers and fans) wasn't finished, and 10 years later— April of 1995— he scored his 41st career victory at the Pomona, California 1/2-mile National event, thus becoming the only rider to win races over a 20-year span. No surprise, Springsteen is a winner in BMW Battle of The Legends races, too, scoring overall wins at Daytona in 1993 and 1996. In Springsteen's case, once a winner, always a winner.

Jay Springsteen has been a favorite of motorcycle racing fans since the mid 1970s.

Dan Mahony

Jay won four TT Nationals in his long and illustrious career.

Dave Friedman

"Springer" leads then-up and comer Scott Parker at the San Jose Mile in 1982.

Dave Friedman

Thirteen of Jay's 41 career wins have come on Mile tracks such as San Jose.

Dan Mahony

AMA Grand National Champion (1976, 1977, 1978)

Winner of 41 AMA Grand National races

Opposite page: Mark Mitchell photo

Greg Jarem

PROFILES

DON VESCO

Fastest Man On Two Wheels. That's a distinction that Don Vesco has held as a motorcycle racer. He has set absolute Motorcycle Land Speed Records for two companies— first Yamaha, then Kawasaki. In the process Vesco has piloted his cigar-shaped, twin-engine streamliner to speeds in excess of 300 miles per hour. When it comes to sprinkling speed on the Salt Flats, few, if any, can do it better than Vesco. But racing in a straight line is only half of Vesco's resume. He was also a respected road racer, competing in many AMA national road races during the 1960s and 1970s. And he always showed up at the track with a smile on his face and a welcome greeting for his friends and competitors. That was Vesco's style then and now, making him a true legend of speed and sportsmanship. An original member of the BMW Battle of The Legends team, Don also continues today in his pursuit of recapturing the motorcycle land speed record.

Vesco rode Yamaha road racers for many years. He is seen here at Loudon in 1968.

Dave Friedman

He was also involved with the Bridgestone factory to develop a competitive race bike.

Dave Friedman

Don has set many motorcycle land speed records over the years at Bonneville.

Dave Friedman

Four time holder of the motorcycle Land Speed Record
1970 (251mph), 1974 (288 mph), 1975 (303 mph), 1978 (318) mph)

Opposite page: Mark Mitchell photo

Greg Jarem

PROFILES

WALTER VILLA

Italy's Walter Villa easily could qualify as the answer to the motorcycle trivia question: Who was the only rider ever to win a Grand Prix world championship for Harley-Davidson? In fact, Villa did it four times, twice in 1976 when he captured both the 250cc and 350cc crowns aboard his Harley-Davidson road race models. Of course the two-stroke machines that Villa rode were nothing like the big-bore vee-twins you see rumbling down the boulevards today, but the point is: When America's premier motorcycle manufacturer wanted to win at Grand Prix racing, it called on one of Italy's finest road racers at the time— Walter Villa— to ride the Aermacchi-built Harley-Davidson bikes. In 1974 Villa came to Daytona to ride a 750cc Kawasaki in the 200-mile race. Unfortunately he experienced trouble early and had to retire. In 1993 Villa came back to Daytona along with several other Europeans to compete in the Daytona Battle of the Legends race, placing eighth overall.

Villa shows his smooth style at the Dutch TT in 1974.

Dave Friedman

Walter won three 250cc World Championships riding Harley-Davidson two strokes.

Dave Friedman

Best known for his Harley-Davidson success, Walter was part of a Daytona assault by Kawasaki in 1974.

Dave Friedman

He came to Daytona in 1974, but his Kawasaki broke on the second lap.

Dave Friedman

Winner of 3 250cc Grand Prix World Championships (1974, 1975, 1976)

Winner of 1 350cc Grand Prix World Championship (1976)

Opposite page: Greg Jarem photo

Greg Jarem

PROFILES

WALTER ZELLER

In Memory Of:
Walter Zeller
1927 - 1995

When Walter Zeller was asked to join the BMW Battle of The Legends for the second-ever race in 1993, he did so graciously and without fanfare. That was his style. Despite his age— he was 65 years old—he competed in the race, and had a wonderful time. The Daytona race culminated a career that saw Zeller earn a gold medal during the 1951 International Six Days Trial (now known as the International Six Days Enduro), three German national championships, plus a memorable ride in the Senior TT at the Isle of Man in 1956. Walter Zeller passed away in 1995, but the spirit of competition that he conveyed throughout his racing career lives on with the Battle of the Legends. Racers such as Walter Zeller will be missed, but certainly they can never be forgotten.

Walter flies past Sulby Bridge on his factory-prepared BMW at the 1956 Isle of Man Senior TT. He finished fourth.

B. R. Nicholls

ISDT gold medal winner (1951)

Winner of 3 German motorcycle championships

Opposite page: Greg Jarem photo

From out of the Past...into the Future

Mark Mitchell photo

1992 R100R

1993 R100R

1994 R1100RS

1995 R1100RS

MACHINES

Battle of the Legends

Racing

1 9 9 2   R 1 0 0 R

BMW R100R

Model used in BMW Battle of The Legends
events in 1992

ENGINE

Type:	Air-cooled, four stroke, opposed 2-cylinder
Bore x stroke:	94.0 mm x 70.6 mm
Displacement:	980 cc
Horsepower:	58 Bhp @ 6500 rpm
Torque:	56.0 lb.-ft. @ 3750 rpm
Compression ratio:	8.5:1
Valve gear:	OHV, push-rod activated
Valves:	1 x 42.0 mm intake / 1 x 40.0 mm exhaust
Valves per cylinder:	Two
Ignition:	Transistorized breakerless
Carburetion:	Two 32 mm Bing constant-velocity with manual choke via variable fuel/air enrichment
Fuel capacity:	5.7 U.S. gallons

FRAME AND SUSPENSION

Frame:	Tubular steel, double front downtubes
Front suspension:	Telescopic fork with progressive spring action, oil dampening with fixed dampening rates
Travel/dimensions:	5.3 inches / 41.4 mm stanchion tube diameter
Rear suspension:	Patented BMW Paralever swingarm shaft drive with single gas-filled shock
Travel / dimensions:	4.3 inches, progressive spring, 6 position preload

BRAKE SYSTEM

Front brakes:	Two 4-piston calipers, wear compensation
Front rotors:	Dual 11.2 inch floating rotors
Rear brake:	One drum brake with dual brake shoes
Rear drum:	Single 7.9 inch drum

WHEELS AND TIRES

Front wheel:	2.50 x 18 MT-H2 patented cross spoke, alloy rim
Rear wheel:	2.50 x 17 MT-H2 patented cross spoke, alloy rim
Front tire:	110/80V - 18 T tubeless
Rear tire:	140/80V - 17 T tubeless

DIMENSIONS

Overall length:	87.0 inches (2210 mm)
Overall width:	39.4 inches (1000 mm) (over mirrors)
Wheelbase:	58.8 inches (1495 mm) (without rider)
Ground clearance:	6.7 inches (170 mm) (with rider)
Seat height:	31.5 inches (800 mm)
Steering head angle:	61 degrees, 30 minutes
Front wheel trail:	3.9 inches (99 mm) (with rider)
Weight - dry:	434 lbs.
Weight - wet:	481 lbs.

BMW R100R
Model used in BMW Battle of The Legends
events in 1993

ENGINE
Type:	Air-cooled, four stroke, opposed 2-cylinder
Bore x stroke:	94.0 mm x 70.6 mm
Displacement:	980 cc
Horsepower:	58 Bhp @ 6500 rpm
Torque:	56.0 lb.-ft. @ 3750 rpm
Compression ratio:	8.5:1
Valve gear:	OHV, push-rod activated
Valves:	1 x 42.0 mm intake / 1 x 40.0 mm exhaust
Valves per cylinder:	Two
Ignition:	Transistorized breakerless
Carburetion:	Two 32 mm Bing constant-velocity with manual choke via variable fuel/air enrichment
Fuel capacity:	5.7 U.S. gallons

FRAME AND SUSPENSION
Frame:	Tubular steel, double front downtubes
Front suspension:	Telescopic fork with progressive spring action, oil dampening with fixed dampening rates
Travel/dimensions:	5.3 inches / 41.4 mm stanchion tube diameter
Rear suspension:	Patented BMW Paralever swingarm shaft drive with single gas-filled shock
Travel / dimensions:	4.3 inches, progressive spring, 6 position preload

BRAKE SYSTEM
Front brakes:	Two 4-piston calipers, wear compensation
Front rotors:	Dual 11.2 inch floating rotors
Rear brake:	One drum brake with dual brake shoes
Rear drum:	Single 7.9 inch drum

WHEELS AND TIRES
Front wheel:	2.50 x 18 MT-H2 patented cross spoke, alloy rim
Rear wheel:	2.50 x 17 MT-H2 patented cross spoke, alloy rim
Front tire:	110/80V - 18 T tubeless
Rear tire:	140/80V - 17 T tubeless

DIMENSIONS
Overall length:	87.0 inches (2210 mm)
Overall width:	39.4 inches (1000 mm) (over mirrors)
Wheelbase:	58.8 inches (1495 mm) (without rider)
Ground clearance:	6.7 inches (170 mm) (with rider)
Seat height:	31.5 inches (800 mm)
Steering head angle:	61 degrees, 30 minutes
Front wheel trail:	3.9 inches (99 mm) (with rider)
Weight - dry:	434 lbs.
Weight - wet:	481 lbs.

BMW R1100RS

Model used in BMW Battle of The Legends events in 1994 and 1995

ENGINE

Type:	Air-cooled, oil-cooled four stroke, opposed 2-cylinder
Bore x stroke:	99.0 mm x 70.5 mm
Displacement:	1085 cc
Horsepower:	90 Bhp @ 7250 rpm
Torque:	69 lb.-ft. @ 5500 rpm
Compression ratio:	10.7:1
Valve gear:	OHC, chain-driven
Valves:	2 x 36.0 mm intake / 2 x 31.0 mm exhaust
Valves per cylinder:	Four
Carburetion/Ignition:	Fuel injection and electronic ignition MA 2.2 controlled by Bosch Motronic
Fuel capacity:	6.07 U.S. gallons

FRAME AND SUSPENSION

Frame:	New 3-section frame concept
Front suspension:	Telelever with central spring strut & progressive spring and damper rates
Travel/dimensions:	4.72 inches / 35 mm fixed tube diameter
Rear suspension:	BMW Paralever & shaft drive, variable rebound dampening
Travel / dimensions:	5.31 inches, progressive spring, 5 positions

BRAKE SYSTEM: BMW/FAG anti-lock brake system ABS II

Front brakes:	Two 4-piston calipers, wear compensation
Front rotors:	Dual 12.0 inch floating rotors
Rear brake:	Hydraulically operated single disc
Rear drum:	Single 11.2 inch diameter fixed rotor

WHEELS AND TIRES

Front wheel:	3.50 x 17 MT-H2 cast alloy, 3-spoke U-profile
Rear wheel:	4.50 x 18 MT-H2 cast alloy, 3-spoke U-profile
Front tire:	120/70 - ZR17 tubeless
Rear tire:	160/60 - ZR18 tubeless

DIMENSIONS

Overall length:	85.6 inches (2175 mm)
Overall width:	26.2 inches (666 mm) (across footrest)
Wheelbase:	57.5 inches (1467 mm) (unladen)
Ground clearance:	6.2 inches (159 mm) (unladen)
Seat height:	31.5 inches (820 - 780 mm) Adjustable
Steering head angle:	65.9 degrees
Front wheel trail:	4.1 inches (104 mm) (unladen)
Weight - dry:	506 lbs.
Weight - wet:	542 lbs.

BMW R1100RS

Model used in BMW Battle of The Legends events in 1995 and 1996

ENGINE

Type:	Air-cooled, oil-cooled four stroke, opposed 2-cylinder
Bore x stroke:	99.0 mm x 70.5 mm
Displacement:	1085 cc
Horsepower:	90 Bhp @ 7250 rpm
Torque:	69 lb.-ft. @ 5500 rpm
Compression ratio:	10.7:1
Valve gear:	OHC, chain-driven
Valves:	2 x 36.0 mm intake / 2 x 31.0 mm exhaust
Valves per cylinder:	Four
Carburetion/Ignition:	Fuel injection and electronic ignition MA 2.2 controlled by Bosch Motronic
Fuel capacity:	6.07 U.S. gallons

FRAME AND SUSPENSION

Frame:	New 3-section frame concept
Front suspension:	Telelever with central spring strut & progressive spring and damper rates
Travel/dimensions:	4.72 inches / 35 mm fixed tube diameter
Rear suspension:	BMW Paralever & shaft drive, variable rebound dampening
Travel / dimensions:	5.31 inches, progressive spring, 5 positions

BRAKE SYSTEM: BMW/FAG anti-lock brake system ABS II

Front brakes:	Two 4-piston calipers, wear compensation
Front rotors:	Dual 12.0 inch floating rotors
Rear brake:	Hydraulically operated single disc
Rear drum:	Single 11.2 inch diameter fixed rotor

WHEELS AND TIRES

Front wheel:	3.50 x 17 MT-H2 cast alloy, 3-spoke U-profile
Rear wheel:	4.50 x 18 MT-H2 cast alloy, 3-spoke U-profile
Front tire:	120/70 - ZR17 tubeless
Rear tire:	160/60 - ZR18 tubeless

DIMENSIONS

Overall length:	85.6 inches (2175 mm)
Overall width:	26.2 inches (666 mm) (across footrest)
Wheelbase:	57.5 inches (1467 mm) (unladen)
Ground clearance:	6.2 inches (159 mm) (unladen)
Seat height:	31.5 inches (820 - 780 mm) Adjustable
Steering head angle:	65.9 degrees
Front wheel trail:	4.1 inches (104 mm) (unladen)
Weight - dry:	506 lbs.
Weight - wet:	542 lbs.

Greg Jarem photo

EVENTS

Battle of the Legends

D A Y T O N A   ' 9 2

The first BMW Battle of The Legends team...from left to right are Mann, Springsteen, Nixon, Reiman, Duhamel, Vesco, Markel, Pridmore, Emde and Roeder.

Reg Pridmore

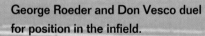
George Roeder and Don Vesco duel for position in the infield.

The two "Number Nines" Springsteen and Nixon "get ready to rumble" (Jay has the black #9).

Former Daytona winners Roger Reiman (55) and Don Emde (25) picked up where they left off back in the seventies. They finished fourth and sixth overall respectively.

"Wow! Did we used to go that fast?" Reiman and Dick Mann compare notes of what it was like to be back on the banks of Daytona.

The inaugural BMW Battle of The Legends event in 1992 was a light-hearted affair with most of the riders in the field getting their first serious racing action in twenty years. Two races were run on the Monday of Bike Week in conjunction with AHRMA's vintage races at the Daytona International Speedway and the best combined score determined the overall finish. Yvon Duhamel was the overall winner.

Daytona 1992 Photos by Don Bok & Greg Jarem

George Roeder

Just like old times! Gary Nixon (9) and Yvon Duhamel (17) doing battle at Daytona with Don Vesco in pursuit. They split the individual race wins and Duhamel came out on top in the overall

Don Emde

Yvon Duhamel, the overall winner of the 1992 BMW Battle of The Legends races.

Close quarters in turn one. Pridmore leads Reiman (55), Roeder (94), Springsteen (9), Emde (25), Duhamel (17) and the rest of the field follows.

The matching red leather BMW racing suits ready for action.

You really didn't have to ask Dick Mann if he had a good time.

Bart Markel

George Roeder (94) at speed. He finished eighth overall.

DAYTONA '93

Jay Springsteen (seated on the bike) came away with the best combined score at the 1993 event. The Legends gathered for this group shot and to offer congratulations to the winner.

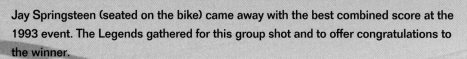

The lineup for one of the two races. Don Castro (11), Roger Reiman (55), Bart Markel (4), Walter Zeller (21) and Reg Pridmore (163) fill out the front row.

Reg Pridmore chases the leaders but still takes a peek to see who is coming up from behind. He finished in sixth place overall.

The largest field of riders to run in the BMW Battle of The Legends was at the 1993 Daytona races. With the crowds growing larger from the previous year, fifteen riders from around the world participated in the event. Joining the American Legends were International stars Phil Read, Hugh Anderson, Walter Villa and Walter Zeller. The identical new BMW R100R "Boxers" sported the new Battle of The Legends graphics on pearl white paint.

Daytona 1993 Photos by Don Bok, Greg Jarem & Mark Mitchell

Jay Springsteen is always in demand by the fans.

BMW's Mark Polk (left) and Phil Capossela (far right) make presentations to Springsteen in the winner's circle after the races.

Yvon Duhamel (17) leads Don Vesco (11), Phil Read (1) and the rest of the pack out onto the service road that leads to the back straightaway.

Don Emde (25) leads Italy's Walter Villa, the former World Road Race Champion. They finished seventh and eighth overall.

The former Superbike Champion Reg Pridmore (163) leads Gary Nixon and the field.

The 1993 Daytona event was David Aldana's first race in the BMW Battle of The Legends series. He won the second race and finished third overall.

Don Vesco (11) and Reg Pridmore (163) race for the lead off the start.

Springsteen leads Nixon.

Seven-time World Champion Phil Read leads fellow Englishman Reg Pridmore.

Hey Jay, this isn't a dirt race! We're not sure what Jay was doing here, but he did put some distance between himself and Gary Nixon.

New Zealand's Hugh Anderson and Don Vesco cool off between races. They finished ninth and tenth respectively.

Germany's Walter Zeller had a great time at Daytona.

The 1992 winner Yvon Duhamel had to "settle" for second overall this year.

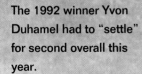

LOUDON, NH '93

David Aldana has the lead, while Yvon Duhamel (17) is caught "dirt tracking" ahead of Nixon, Emde, Vesco and the field.

Don Castro welcomes three-time Daytona winner Dick Klamfoth to the BMW Battle of The Legends series. In his career, Klamfoth won twice at the old Belknap track in nearby Laconia.

Don Castro

The summer of 1993 saw the first BMW Battle of The Legends race somewhere other than Daytona. That summer the Legends traveled to historic Loudon, New Hampshire to take part in a vintage car & motorcycle race over the Fourth of July weekend. To add some variety, riders from three different eras were invited to ride. David Aldana, Don Castro and Don Emde made up the "Under 50" group; Yvon Duhamel, Gary Nixon and Roger Reiman were in the "Over 50" group, and Dick Klamfoth, Bart Markel, Dick Mann and Don Vesco were in "Over 57."

The Three Dons...Emde (25) leads Vesco and Castro.

Roger Reiman (55) leads Dick Mann. Like Klamfoth, Mann was also a two-time winner at Laconia.

Bart Markel rode with Vesco, Mann and Klamfoth in the Over-57 division.

Loudon race photos by Chuck Dearborn.

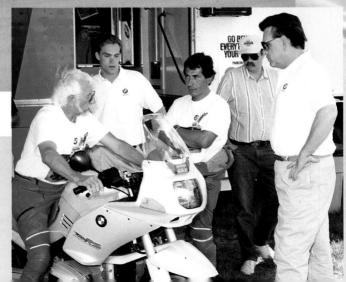

Overall winner was David Aldana who swept both races during the Loudon vintage motorsports race weekend.

Don Vesco tries on a stock R1100RS for size while David Dampf (to Vesco's left), David Aldana and Richard Dampf look on.

The BMW "Paddock" at Loudon.

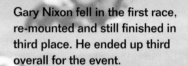

Gary Nixon fell in the first race, re-mounted and still finished in third place. He ended up third overall for the event.

BMW Technicians Chuck Dearborn (left) and Tom deMange pose with Dick Mann and Dearborn's Matchless G50, the same model Dick won the 1963 AMA championship with.

Don Castro (11) holds off Dick Klamfoth in the infield section of the new Loudon Super Speedway.

Duhamel leads Aldana at this point, with Nixon, Emde and Reiman in pursuit. Aldana would eventually get by for the win.

Second place finisher, Yvon Duhamel

"Bad Bart" Markel gets ready for action, while Buddy Gerber stands by.

Fifth place finisher Don Emde (middle) reviews the action with Roger Reiman who was fourth.

DAYTONA '94

David Aldana nailed down the overall victory in the 1994 events at Daytona.

Two days of hard racing and still friends!

The pace picked up considerably in 1994 with the change to the new R1100RS sportbikes from BMW. Here David Aldana leads Springsteen, Nixon, Duhamel, Pridmore, Emde and Reiman.

Daytona 1994

There were some big changes with the 1994 Daytona event from the previous year. The format saw the return to just ten riders and the switch to BMW's new R1100RS sportbike. With top speeds around the banks of Daytona jumping from about 115 to 135, the racing got a lot more serious.

Daytona 1994 photos by Greg Jarem

Roger Reiman (left), Reg Pridmore (center) and Don Emde (right) cool off after one of the races. They finished sixth, fourth and seventh overall.

Clear the way. Gary Nixon heads for the track. Richard DeZago is holding the tent up.

David Aldana

BMW Vice President of Motorcycle Operations Phil Capossela greets the 1994 Battle of The Legends Grand Marshal John Surtees.

"I was just like this and saved it!"

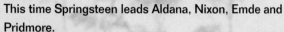

This time Springsteen leads Aldana, Nixon, Emde and Pridmore.

Reg Pridmore gives Dave Despain his report of the action for the video and television programs that covered the races.

Don Castro gives his perspective.

Yvon Duhamel ended up second overall for the second year in a row. He did win one of the two races.

One of the highlights of the BMW Battle of The Legends series is the chance for the fans to talk to their heroes of the past and get an autograph or two.

Kurt Liebmann, a long time BMW rider and supporter was a member of the 1994 team at Daytona. He finished eighth overall.

The two number elevens, Don Vesco (on the outside) and Don Castro race into turn one.

Dick Mann (left), Dick Klamfoth (middle) and George Roeder share a fun moment at the autograph session held at the American Mechanics Institute in Daytona the day before the races.

SEARS POINT '94

Nine of the ten riders at Sears Point posed after the races for the group photo. Don Castro was missing due to a fall in the final race.

Reg Pridmore

BMW's Tom deMange and Roger Reiman discuss the situation.

The Legends get ready for action. This was the first-ever race for many of the Legends at Sears Point.

SEARS POINT 1994

The Summer of 1994 saw the BMW Battle of The Legends series head to the Sears Point Raceway north of San Francisco, California for a two-day event. New for Sears Point were two riders in the series...Walt Fulton and Eddie Mulder... and new racing leathers for the team. A few of the rider's suits needed some adjustments, so this event saw a sprinkling of different outfits. The weather was great and the first West Coast appearance of the Legends was a success.

Sears Point 1994 photos by Chuck Dearborn & Mark Mitchell

Don Emde (opposite page) narrowly leads Gary Nixon and Yvon Duhamel on day one.

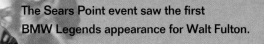

The Sears Point event saw the first BMW Legends appearance for Walt Fulton.

First-time Legend rider Eddie Mulder leads Don Vesco and Don Castro.

David Aldana (13) and Reg Pridmore (opposite page) traded wins at Sears Point with Aldana coming out on top overall.

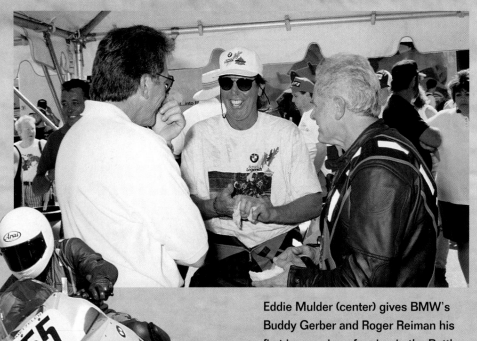

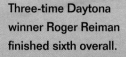

Eddie Mulder (center) gives BMW's Buddy Gerber and Roger Reiman his first impression of racing in the Battle of The Legends.

Three-time Daytona winner Roger Reiman finished sixth overall.

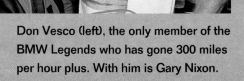

Don Vesco (left), the only member of the BMW Legends who has gone 300 miles per hour plus. With him is Gary Nixon.

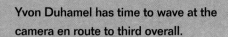

Yvon Duhamel has time to wave at the camera en route to third overall.

Don Emde (left) congratulates his old BSA teammate David Aldana on his overall win.

Don Vesco

Don Castro took a nasty looking tumble in the second race. Fortunately, he did not suffer any serious injuries and was back in action the following March at Daytona. David Aldana gives Castro a lift back to the pits.

D A Y T O N A   ' 9 5

Daytona 1995 was the last race for the white R1100RS race bikes. Here the team poses with a new 1995 model in blue like the Legends would begin riding at the Mid-Ohio race the following July.

(above) Don Emde (25) leads Yvon Duhamel, Jay Springsteen and Walt Fulton (66).

Yvon Duhamel leads Jay Springsteen (now riding with #1), Roger Reiman (55), Gary Nixon (9) and David Aldana (partially hidden).

Jay Springsteen (1), Don Castro (now sporting #5), Roger Reiman (55) and new Legend rider Jody Nicholas get ready for the start.

DAYTONA 1995

Change was again in the wind at Daytona for 1995. Due to the continuing popularity of the series, the 1995 schedule called for three races on three separate days at the Speedway. Jody Nicholas, star of the 1960's and 1970's made his BMW Battle of The Legends debut and finished in 6th place overall. Another change for 1995 was the use of the full Daytona road race course rather than the abbreviated course the Legends had used previously.

Daytona 1995 photos by Mark Mitchell

Gary Nixon

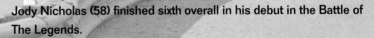

Jody Nicholas (58) finished sixth overall in his debut in the Battle of The Legends.

Jay Springsteen obliges a fan.

Springsteen, Duhamel and Fulton battle on the banks.

Roger Reiman still has a loyal following after all these years.

1967 Daytona winner Gary Nixon took the overall victory with two wins and a fifth in the three races in 1995.

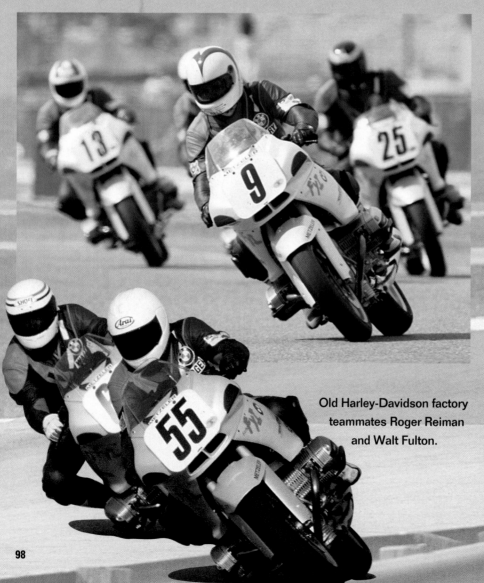

Yvon Duhamel

Gary Nixon and his buddy Jay Springsteen.

Old Harley-Davidson factory teammates Roger Reiman and Walt Fulton.

Don Vesco (left) tries to explain to Walt Fulton and Don Emde what road racing is like with just one eye. He lost the use of his left eye the previous winter when he was hit by a rock while sitting in the grandstands at a car race .

Eddie Mulder was popular in his first ride at Daytona in about twenty years.

David Aldana leads the group out of the International Horseshoe turn with Springer in pursuit.

MID-OHIO '95

Eddie Mulder (12) leads Roger Reiman, Chris Draayer, Mark Brelsford (hidden) and Walt Fulton. Mulder had his best finish to date in the series with a fourth in the second race.

The Legends and attending Legends Emeritus gather after a successful weekend of racing. Adding his congratulations is Kevin Westfall, President of BMW Financial Services.

First time Legends competitor Chris Draayer quickly made friends with fans of all ages.

Legends ready to race.

Mark Brelsford was also a first timer in the Legends competition at Mid-Ohio. In the background Don Vesco chats with Bart Markel.

In the Summer of 1995, the series moved to the Mid-Ohio Sports Car course in Lexington, Ohio. Two new riders from years past joined the series at this event. Mark Brelsford, the 1972 AMA Grand National Champion rode his first motorcycle race since racing injuries brought his career to a halt in 1974. Another rider joining the series, who had experienced serious injuries in his career was Chris Draayer, the 1966 AMA Rookie of The Year.

Mid-Ohio 1995 photos by Chuck Dearborn

Don Emde (25) leads Duhamel, Nixon, Reiman and Mulder.

Yvon Duhamel leads Walt Fulton down the front straightaway.

Don Emde leads the field. He won the second leg at Mid-Ohio and ended up third overall.

Yvon Duhamel turned a 2nd and a 3rd place finish into the overall victory at Mid-Ohio.

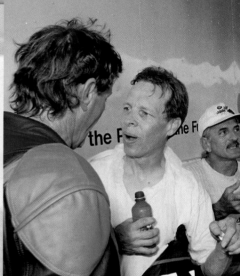

Eddie Mulder and Mark Brelsford discuss the action, with Duhamel and Vesco doing the same in the background.

Yvon Duhamel leads Eddie Mulder, Gary Nixon, Roger Reiman and Chris Draayer.

Number 77 is first time BMW Legend Chris Draayer. He finished fifth overall, a great achievement for a first race effort in almost thirty years. Along side is Gary Nixon.

Chris Draayer, who lost his left arm in a racing accident in 1967, brought with him a special device to assist him on the track. He explains how to install it to BMW technicians Frank Zabriskie, Jack Del Pizzo and Richard Dampf.

Fans standing patiently in line to get a poster or shirt signed by the Legends.

DAYTONA '96

The winner of the 1995 Daytona Battle of The Legends Gary Nixon leads Jay Springsteen, Walt Fulton, Yvon Duhamel and Roger Reiman.

BMW's Richard Dampf (on the motorcycle) shares a moment with the Legends. The red, white and blue jackets were special editions commemorating BMW's role in the Summer Games of the 1996 Olympics.

Yvon Duhamel (opposite page) sprints into Daytona's turn one with Jay Springsteen (1), Walt Fulton (66), Roger Reiman, Gary Nixon (9) and Don Emde (25) in pursuit. Jay became the first two-time Daytona winner in the series in 1996.

TT ace Eddie Mulder gives his impression of racing at Daytona.

DAYTONA 1996

The 1996 BMW Battle of The Legends races at Daytona saw some of the closest and best racing in the series to date. All of the ten riders in the field were stuck together in a pack for most of the week. To the delight of the large crowd of race fans, at times the field would run around the banking virtually as one. At the end of the week, Gary Nixon and Jay Springsteen ended up tied for the most points. Springsteen became the first two-time winner of the Legends events at Daytona after he was declared the overall winner, having beaten Nixon in the final leg.

Daytona 1996 photos by Mark Mitchell

At the annual BMW press conference, AHRMA's Executive Director Jeff Smith welcomes the legendary Geoff Duke as 1996 Grand Marshall.

Don Emde leads Springsteen en route to a fifth place overall finish.

Mark Brelsford raced at Daytona for the first time since 1974 and won the first of the three legs of the 1996 Daytona event.

Eddie Mulder (12) leads Fulton and Reiman. Although he wound up ninth overall, he was close to the front all week long.

Reg Pridmore rode hard to finish third overall.

The Legends riders have developed a great following and are always happy to sign a poster, hat or shirt for a fan.

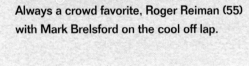

Always a crowd favorite, Roger Reiman (55) with Mark Brelsford on the cool off lap.

DAYTONA ★

Across the line lap after lap, the 1996 Legends riders were the closest matched group in the series yet. Every race was decided by just a wheel length at the most.

Yvon Duhamel won the third leg of the 1996 Daytona event.

Chris Draayer (77) chases Roger Reiman. Chris fell hard in race two and was not able to return to action that week.

Reg Pridmore gives Jay Springsteen a lesson in dragging a knee through a turn.

Walt Fulton

M I D - O H I O   ' 9 6

The 1996 BMW Legends "Summer Team" for the Mid-Ohio race.

The BMW crew during a quiet moment. From left to right are Dan Carson, Chuck Dearborn, Frank Zabriskie, Richard Dampf and Michael Hand.

Reg Pridmore fell in the first race but still ended up fifth overall for the weekend.

Reg Pridmore leads David Aldana in the second leg. Aldana got by for the win to secure the overall event victory.

For the second year in a row, the BMW Battle of The Legends returned to the Mid-Ohio Sports Car course north of Columbus. The crowd was bigger yet from the previous year and the race action was close and fast. The 1996 Mid-Ohio race saw the return of Don Castro and Jody Nicholas to action after brief layoffs.

Mid-Ohio 1996 photos by Chuck Dearborn & Mark Mitchell

Don Castro

Eddie Mulder leads the way in race two ahead of Walt Fulton and Reg Pridmore.

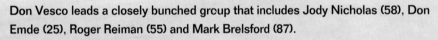

Don Vesco leads a closely bunched group that includes Jody Nicholas (58), Don Emde (25), Roger Reiman (55) and Mark Brelsford (87).

Don Emde won one of the two legs at Mid-Ohio for the second year in a row. He wound up second overall behind Aldana.

Jody Nicholas leads Don Emde in race two.

David Aldana picked up his fourth overall race win at Mid-Ohio.

Jody Nicholas ended up with a pair of sixth place finishes which gave him sixth place overall.

Eddie Mulder (left) and Walt Fulton cool down with a rundown of "how it was" out on the race track.

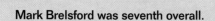

Mark Brelsford was seventh overall.

BMW

METZELER

FORBES FYI

AHRMA

SPONSORS

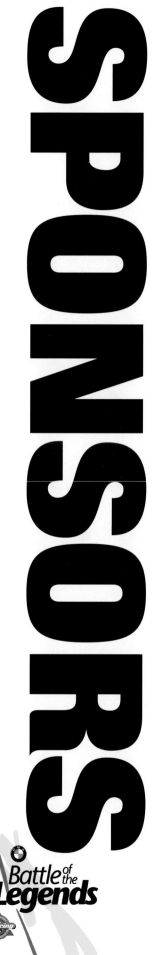

Battle of the Legends

Mark Mitchell photo

113

S P O N S O R S

From left: Tom deMange, David Dampf, Chuck Dearborn, Richard Dampf, Bud Gerber.

THOUGHTS FROM BEHIND THE SCENES

Wandering into the BMW pit area at any Battle of the Legends event was similar to happening upon an oasis in the middle of a desert. Crisp white tents bore the distinctive BMW logo, rows of highly polished BMW motorcycles glistened in the sun, and cases of neatly organized tools and supplies stood at the ready.

Bustling about the area were five freshly scrubbed gentlemen, all outfitted in tan khakis and spotless blue shirts that bore their names in embroidered script - Richard, Chuck, Tom, Bud and David. The BMW Battle of the Legends Motorcycle Technicians. While the Legends enjoyed the spotlight, these fellows worked behind the scenes for months preparing the BMWs for competition.

Shortly after Thanksgiving, when the bikes arrived in Port Newark, Jersey City, NJ from Germany, this highly dedicated team of technicians, led by BMW Motorcycles' National Event/ Fleet Manager Richard Dampf, worked tirelessly on weekends and weeknights to put mileage on the motorcycles and ready them for Daytona. By Christmas, each bike had logged approximately 600 miles.

During the race week, the technicians busily attended to every detail of every motorcycle, working with each Legend rider to ensure their comfort and safety. At the start line, they dutifully shielded Legends from the sun with oversized BMW umbrellas, while at the finish, they greeted each competitor with pats on the back and wide smiles.

A very close knit group of old friends, the technicians included former roadracer Chuck Dearborn, 49, who owns Cycle Engineering in Norwood, NJ; Tom deMange, 56, also a former roadracer with more than 30 years of experience in motorcycling - from roadracing to preparation of vintage bikes; Bud Gerber, 57, a massage therapist and avid motorcyclist who worked as a member of autoracing pit crews; and 24-year-old David Dampf, Richard's son, who works as a road service representative for the Automobile Club of New York. David shares his father's passion for motorcycles and racing. Dearborn, deMange and Gerber have known each other for more than 30 years, while Dearborn and Richard Dampf can trace their friendship all the way back to elementary school.

There are several other BMW technicians who were part of the team of technicians who kept the finely tuned BMWs in good working order. They included Charlie Johnson, Frank Zabriskie, Jehd Webster, Gery Torok, Norman Hedlund, and Ed Mitchell.

Bud Gerber:

"Having ridden for more than 25 years, I am in complete awe of the talent these men possess. What they're able to achieve on a street bike is amazing, and they're actually having as much fun as they did during their active racing days. The Legends are such gentlemen, I feel humbled just to be in their company. I truly believe that the BMW Battle of the Legends was the only event during Bike Week in which the fans were the real winners."

Tom deMange:

"I started riding in 1962 and remember attending races in Hagerstown, MD; Reading, PA; York PA; and Laconia. To a 22-year old street rider, these were the most exciting events in the world. My heroes were the racers out on the track. Thirty years later, Richard Dampf offered me the opportunity to become part of the Legends crew. I quickly discovered they were not only my heroes and outstanding racers, but also a group of men who are supreme gentlemen. It's gratifying to see them receiving the recognition they deserve. Both on and off the track, they are true Legends."

Chuck Dearborn:

"As a roadracer in the '70s, I had an opportunity to race on the same team with Reg Pridmore and Kurt Liebmann. I used to watch the flat track racers in awe. They were the big boys. Working with the BMW Battle of the Legends afforded me the opportunity to be reunited with the guys I watched and to get to know them on a more personal level. It was a rare privilege to assemble a group of racers of this caliber to have some fun together without all of the rivalries of the past."

David Dampf:

"Although I was not familiar with any of the Legends before my involvement in the event, since I am of a different generation, I was amazed at their talent and the incredible respect they were shown by so many fans. Participating in the BMW Battle of the Legends was certainly a high point in my life and I couldn't be more proud of my father for organizing and coordinating all of the behind-the-scenes details of this fantastic event. His hard work will long be remembered."

Klaus Becker came all the way from BMW headquarters in Germany to watch the action. With him is BMW's Phil Capossela.

The technical support for the inaugural BMW Battle of The Legends at Daytona in 1992. From left: Jehd Webster, Bud Gerber, Charlie Johnson, Richard Dampf, Norman Hedlund and Chuck Dearborn.

Richard Dampf gives one of the race bikes a last minute fill-up and avoids a potentially embarrassing moment for BMW.

Frank Zabriskie (right) with Buddy Gerber

Ed Mitchell always brought his smile and good humor to the BMW Legends events.

Tom deMange rolls a bike through tech at Sears Point while the boss, Richard Dampf gives the machine a visual inspection of his own.

The senior Dampf has the wrenches out, while son David watches.

Chuck Dearborn (left) preps a bike with input from Marvin Kirkpatrick and Jerald Munson.

Richard Dampf is as good with a plate of cookies as he is with the wrenches!

An impressive site at each of the Legends races is the unloading of the bikes from the huge BMW hauler.

Scott Arigot, BMW's Motorcycle Marketing Manager gives rider Walt Fulton something to chuckle about while Public Relations Director Renae Biale looks on.

Legends Emeritus Dick Klamfoth leads a group of riders around the banks of Daytona during the popular BMW Pace Ride.

A BMW owner on the grid with the Legends gets ready for the Pace Ride.

Roger Reiman spends a moment with a proud BMW owner, Ryder McClure.

The 1996 Daytona races were the 20th anniversary of BMW's Superbike win at Daytona. BMW's Motorcycle Group Vice President Phil Capossela offers his congratulations to Udo Gietl, the person who headed up BMW's racing program in the 1970's.

The Metzeler people did a great job throughout the series making sure the Legends had good traction.

Just about every time a Legends rider came off the track a Metzeler tire technician was there to meet him. Here Jeff Johnston checks the pressure on a 1994 R1100RS.

METZELER

Metzeler guys take their jobs very seriously and were always looking for input from the riders.

While BMW's Bud Gerber (left) and Frank Zabriskie tend to the motorcycle, Metzeler's Cory Jonson is keeping track of the tire status.

Forbes FyI

At Daytona 1996, Robert Forbes presented a $3,000 check from Forbes FYI Magazine to Sue Slate and Gin Shear of the Women's Motorcyclist Foundation for the Pony Express Tour '96 to raise funds for breast cancer research. They later went on to raise almost $300,000, which was donated to the Susan G. Komen Foundation.

Robert Forbes in the back with all the Legends in victory lane at Daytona in 1994.

One of the most identifiable elements of the Forbes organization is their famous balloons. At right, this is about all it could do during the windy 1995 Vintage Motorcycle Days events.

No doubt keeping the program on schedule, AHRMA's Executive Director Jeff Smith (at right) makes a point to BMW's Richard Dampf (middle) and Rob Mitchell. The Battle of The Legends events are held in conjunction with the vintage races that draw literally hundreds of entrants to each event.

AHRMA's Technical Director Jack Turner filled in as an announcer at the 1994 Sears Point event. Here he chats with race winner David Aldana in the Winner's Circle.

At an AHRMA vintage motorcycle race you'll see plenty of motorcycles of days-gone-by, such as this vintage BMW ridden by Ralph Auer. He was the AHRMA National Champion in Class C and Pre-40 Class in 1996.

Mark Mitchell photo

APPENDIX

Battle of the Legends

R A C E   R E S U L T S

DAYTONA 1992
1. Yvon Duhamel (2-1)
2. Jay Springsteen (3-2)
3. Gary Nixon (1-5)
4. Roger Reiman (4-3)
5. Reg Pridmore (5-4)
6. Don Emde (6-6)
7. Don Vesco (8-7)
8. George Roeder (7-8)
9. Bart Markel (10-9)
10. Dick Mann (9-10)

DAYTONA 1993
1. Jay Springsteen (1-2)
2. Yvon Duhamel (2-3)
3. David Aldana (3-1)
4. Gary Nixon (4-4)
5. Phil Read (5-5)
6. Reg Pridmore (6-6)
7. Don Emde (7-8)
8. Walter Villa (10-7)
9. Hugh Anderson (8-9)
10. Don Vesco (9-11)
11. George Roeder (11-12)
12. Roger Reiman (14-10)
13. Don Castro (12-13)
14. Bart Markel (13-14)
15. Walter Zeller (15-15)

LOUDON, NH 1993
1. David Aldana (1-1)
2. Yvon Duhamel (2-2)
3. Gary Nixon (3-3)
4. Roger Reiman (5-4)
5. Don Emde (4-5)
6. Don Vesco (6-6)
7. Dick Klamfoth (7-7)
8. Don Castro (9-8)
9. Dick Mann (8-9)
10. Bart Markel (10-10)

DAYTONA 1994
1. David Aldana (2-1)
2. Yvon Duhamel (1-3)
3. Jay Springsteen (3-2)
4. Reg Pridmore (6-4)
5. Gary Nixon (4-6)
6. Roger Reiman (7-5)
7. Don Emde (5-7)
8. Kurt Liebmann (8-8)
9. Don Vesco (10-9)
10. Don Castro (9-10)

SEARS POINT, CA 1994
1. David Aldana (2-1)
2. Reg Pridmore (1-2)
2. Yvon Duhamel (5-3)
4. Gary Nixon (4-4)
5. Don Emde (3-5)
6. Roger Reiman (6-6)
7. Eddie Mulder (10-7)
8. Don Vesco (7-8)
9. Walt Fulton (8-9)
10. Don Castro (9-10)

DAYTONA 1995
1. Gary Nixon (1-1-5)
2. Jay Springsteen (3-4-2)
3. Yvon Duhamel (4-5-1)
4. Roger Reiman (4-3-3)
5. David Aldana (2-2-6)
6. Jody Nicholas (8-8-4)
7. Walt Fulton (7-7-7)
8. Don Emde (6-6-10)
9. Don Castro (10-11-8)
10. Eddie Mulder (11-9-9)
11. Don Vesco (9-10-11)

MID-OHIO 1995
1. Yvon Duhamel (3-2)
2. Roger Reiman (1-5)
3. Don Emde (7-1)
4. Gary Nixon (5-3)
5. Chris Draayer (4-6)
6. David Aldana (2-10)
7. Eddie Mulder (10-4)
8. Walt Fulton (6-6)
9. Mark Brelsford (8-7)
10. Don Vesco (9-9)

DAYTONA 1996
1. Jay Springsteen (6-1-2)
2. Gary Nixon (2-3-4)
3. Reg Pridmore (3-5-3)
4. Yvon Duhamel (7-4-1)
5. Don Emde (8-2-5)
6. Walt Fulton (3-6-6)
7. Mark Brelsford (1-8-8)
8. Roger Reiman (5-7-7)
9. Eddie Mulder (10-9-9)
10. Chris Draayer (9-10-DNS)

MID-OHIO 1996
1. David Aldana (2-1)
2. Don Emde (1-5)
3. Eddie Mulder (4-3)
4. Walt Fulton (3-4)
5. Reg Pridmore (8-2)
6. Jody Nicholas (6-6)
7. Mark Brelsford (7-7)
8. Roger Reiman (8-8)
9. Don Vesco (9-9)
10. Don Castro (10-10)

OVERALL VICTORIES OF BMW BATTLE OF THE LEGENDS EVENTS

(Best overall score in races held at each event)

David Aldana	4
Yvon Duhamel	2
Jay Springsteen	2
Gary Nixon	1

INDIVIDUAL RACE WINS

David Aldana	6
Yvon Duhamel	4
Gary Nixon	3
Don Emde	2
Jay Springsteen	2
Mark Brelsford	1
Reg Pridmore	1
Roger Reiman	1

Don Bok

BMW BATTLE OF THE LEGENDS SERIES POINT STANDINGS

Event Code:
1=Daytona 92; 2=Daytona 93; 3=Loudon 93; 4=Daytona 94; 5=Sears Point 94;
6=Daytona 95; 7=Mid-Ohio 95; 8=Daytona 96; 9=Mid-Ohio 96

(15 Points for 1st overall, 1 point for 15th overall)

Points Scored:

		Event									
		1	2	3	4	5	6	7	8	9	T
1.	Yvon Duhamel	15	14	14	14	13	13	15	12	-	110
2.	Gary Nixon	13	12	13	11	12	15	12	14	-	102
3.	Don Emde	10	9	11	9	11	8	13	11	14	96
4.	David Aldana	-	13	15	15	15	11	10	-	15	94
5.	Roger Reiman	12	4	12	10	10	12	14	8	8	90
6.	Reg Pridmore	11	10	-	12	14	-	-	13	11	71
(tie)	Jay Springsteen	14	15	-	13	-	14	-	15	-	71
8.	Don Vesco	9	6	10	7	8	5	6	-	7	58
9.	Walt Fulton	-	-	-	-	7	8	8	10	12	45
10.	Eddie Mulder	-	-	-	-	9	6	9	7	13	44
11.	Don Castro	-	3	7	6	6	7	-	-	6	35
12.	Mark Brelsford	-	-	-	-	-	-	7	9	9	25
13.	Jody Nicholas	-	-	-	-	-	10	-	-	10	20
14.	Chris Draayer	-	-	-	-	-	-	11	6	-	17
15.	Bart Markel	7	2	6	-	-	-	-	-	-	15
16.	Dick Mann	6	-	8	-	-	-	-	-	-	14
17.	George Roeder	8	5	-	-	-	-	-	-	-	13
18.	Phil Read	-	11	-	-	-	-	-	-	-	11
19.	Dick Klamfoth	-	-	9	-	-	-	-	-	-	9
20.	Kurt Liebmann	-	-	-	8	-	-	-	-	-	8
(tie)	Walter Villa	-	8	-	-	-	-	-	-	-	8
22.	Hugh Anderson	-	7	-	-	-	-	-	-	-	7
23.	Walter Zeller	-	1	-	-	-	-	-	-	-	1

WANT TO KNOW WHO RODE WHAT BIKE?

BMW Machine Identification Numbers

DAYTONA 1992
R100R
(Black or Purple)

VIN #	RIDER
0280012	Reiman
0280055	Pridmore
0280058	Springsteen
0280034	Nixon
0280010	Emde
0280011	Roeder
0280056	Markel
0280057	DuHamel
0280009	Mann
0280013	Vesco
0280059	Backup bike
0280008	Backup bike

DAYTONA 1994-1995 & SEARS POINT
R1100RS (White)

VIN #	RIDER
0311298	Aldana
0311316	Pridmore
0311318	Springsteen
0311266	Castro
0311302	Fulton
0311301	Reiman
0311297	DuHamel
0311315	Mulder
0311295	Nixon
0311620	Liebmann
0311300	Emde
0311294	Vesco

DAYTONA & LOUDON 1993
R100R (White)

VIN #	RIDER
0280472	Vesco
0280580	Zeller
0280582	DuHamel
0280563	Aldana
0280462	Pridmore
0280441	Nixon
0280451	Anderson
0280453	Emde
0280464	Villa
0280527	Read
0280528	Reiman
0280530	Castro
0280421	Springsteen
0280533	Markel
0280529	Roeder
0280581	Backup bike
0280566	Backup bike

MID-OHIO 1995-1996 & DAYTONA 1996
R1100RS (Blue)

VIN #	RIDER
0311945	Pridmore
0311955	Nixon
0311957	Springsteen
0311958	Mulder
0311953	Brelsford
0311960	DuHamel
0311961	Emde
0311959	Fulton
0311962	Reiman
0311975	Backup bike
0311976	Backup bike
0311956	Draayer

OUT-TAKES

Millie Horky gives David Aldana an idea of what it is like to ride with one eye, as Don Vesco had to adjust to in 1995.

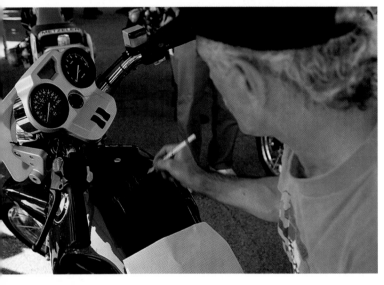

Each of the BMW Legends race bikes were signed by the riders and the autographs were later traced over by a professional sign painter.

Smile, you're on candid camera!

Godspeed Walter.

Too bad everyone was always so serious!

Picture of the Legends getting their picture taken.

Roger Reiman sums up what it was like to ride in the BMW Battle of The Legends.

Everywhere the Legends went, cameras and microphones were rolling.

Don Emde's dad Floyd tries to recruit a new rider for the Legends series.

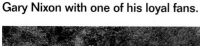
Gary Nixon with one of his loyal fans.

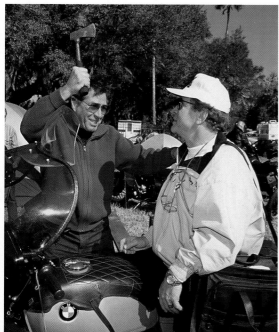

BMW's Buddy Gerber gives Don Vesco the royal treatment.

Thanks to Richard Dampf and everyone at BMW, AHRMA, Forbes FYI and Metzeler for five great years.

The Legends

Battle of the **Legends**